Slippers for the Family

It's easy to crochet cozy footwear for everyone in the family with these 10 versatile designs and the sizing guide on pages 26-27. Use them for quick gifts all through the year — or make festive versions for the holidays. Some have optional sock cuffs for extra warmth.

LOOK FOR THE CAMERA

in our instructions and watch our technique videos made just for you! **www. LeisureArts.com/6628**

LEISURE ARTS, INC. • Maumelle, Arkansas

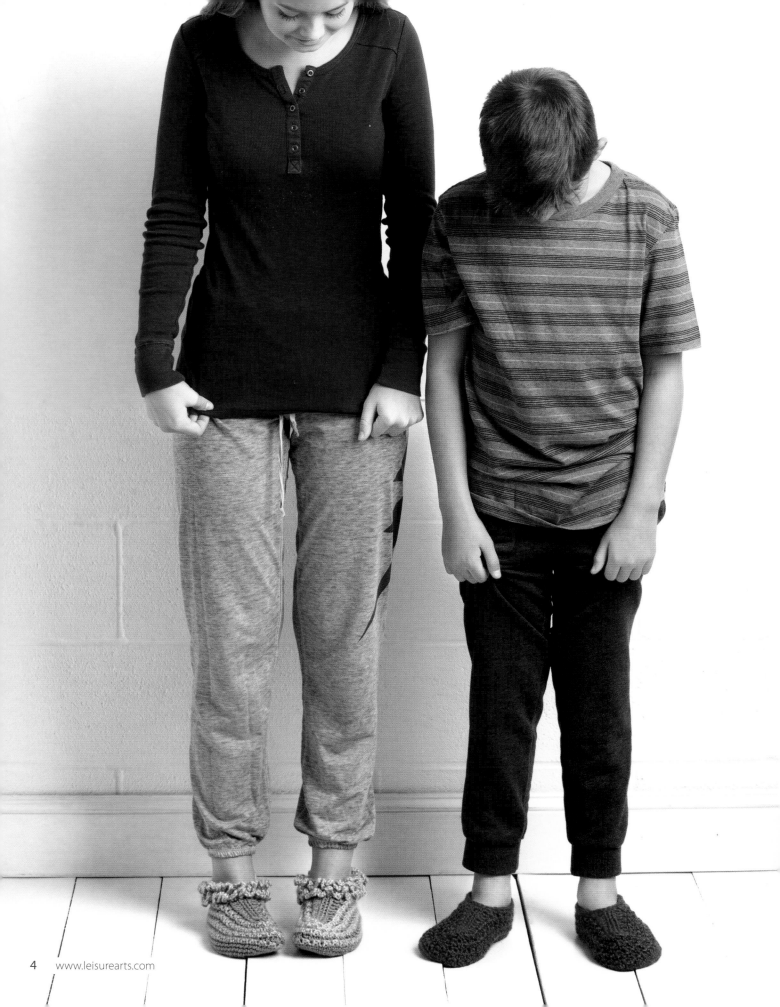

Elf Shoes

Optional Sock Cuffs shown on page 8.

■■□□□ EASY

GAUGE INFORMATION

In pattern,
   7 dc = 2" (5 cm),
   7 rows/rnds = 4" (10 cm)
Gauge Swatch: 2" wide x 4" high
   (5 cm x 10 cm)
Ch 9.
Row 1: Dc in fourth ch from hook
(**3 skipped chs count as first dc**) and
in each ch across: 7 dc.
Rows 2-7: Ch 3 (**counts as first dc**),
turn; dc in next dc and in each dc
across.
Finish off.

ELF SHOE (Make 2)
TOE

Rnd 1 (Right side)**:** With Main Color,
make an adjustable loop to form a
ring *(Figs. 1a-d, page 29)*; ch 2, (hdc,
sc, hdc, dc) in ring; join with slip st to
top of beginning ch-2: 5 sts.

Note: Loop a short piece of yarn
around any stitch to mark Rnd 1 as
right side.

Rnd 2: Ch 3 (**counts as first dc, now
and throughout**), dc in same st as
joining, hdc in next hdc, sc in next sc,
hdc in next hdc, 2 dc in last dc; join
with slip st to first dc: 7 sts.

Rnd 3: Ch 3, dc in same st as joining,
hdc in next dc, sc in next 3 sts, hdc in
next dc, 2 dc in last dc; join with slip st
to first dc: 9 sts.

SHOPPING LIST

Yarn (Medium Weight) **4 MEDIUM**
**[4 ounces, 235 yards
(113 grams, 215 meters) per skein]:**
Elf Shoes
☐ Main Color - 1 skein
☐ Contrasting Color - 14{15-18-21}
   yards/13{13.5-16.5-19} meters
Sock Cuffs
☐ Color A (Red) - 30{35-60-70}
   yards/27.5{32-55-64} meters
☐ Color B (Yellow) - 4{6-8-10}
   yards/3.5{5.5-7.5-9} meters

Crochet Hook
☐ Size H (5 mm)
   or size needed for gauge

Additional Supplies
☐ Safety pin
☐ Yarn needle

SIZE INFORMATION

Child Size	Finished Length	
Small	5¾"	(14.5 cm)
Medium	7"	(18 cm)
Large	8"	(20.5 cm)
Extra Large	9"	(23 cm)

Size Note: We have printed the
instructions for the sizes in different
colors to make it easier for you to find:
• Size Small in Brown
• Size Medium in Purple
• Size Large in Red
• Size Extra Large in Blue
Instructions in Black apply to all sizes.

Rnd 4: Ch 3, dc in same st as joining and in next dc, hdc in next hdc, sc in next 3 sc, hdc in next hdc, dc in next dc, 2 dc in last dc; join with slip st to first dc: 11 sts.

Rnd 5: Ch 3, dc in same st as joining and in next 2 dc, hdc in next hdc, sc in next 3 sc, hdc in next hdc, dc in next 2 dc, 2 dc in last dc; join with slip st to first dc: 13 sts.

Rnd 6: Ch 3, dc in same st as joining and in next 3 dc, hdc in next hdc, sc in next 3 sc, hdc in next hdc, dc in next 3 dc, 2 dc in last dc; join with slip st to first dc: 15 sts.

SIZE SMALL ONLY
Rnd 7: Ch 3, 2 dc in next dc, dc in next 2 dc, 2 dc in next dc, ★ dc in next st, 2 dc in next st, dc in next 2 sts, 2 dc in next st; repeat from ★ once **more**; join with slip st to first dc, do **not** finish off: 21 dc.

SIZE MEDIUM ONLY
Rnd 7: Ch 3, dc in same st as joining, (dc in next st, 2 dc in next st) around; join with slip st to first dc: 23 dc.

Rnd 8: Ch 3, dc in next dc and in each dc around; join with slip st to first dc, do **not** finish off.

SIZE LARGE ONLY
Rnd 7: Ch 3, 2 dc in next dc, dc in next 2 dc, 2 dc in next dc, ★ dc in next st, 2 dc in next st, dc in next 2 sts, 2 dc in next st; repeat from ★ once **more**; join with slip st to first dc, do **not** finish off: 21 dc.

Rnd 8: Ch 3, (dc in next 4 dc, 2 dc in next dc) around; join with slip st to first dc, do **not** finish off: 25 dc.

SIZE EXTRA LARGE ONLY
Rnd 7: Ch 3, dc in same st as joining, (dc in next st, 2 dc in next st) around; join with slip st to first dc: 23 dc.

Rnd 8: Ch 3, dc in next 2 dc, (2 dc in next dc, dc in next 4 dc) around; join with slip st to first dc, do **not** finish off: 27 dc.

FOOT
Rnd 1 (Trim): 🎥 Place loop from hook onto safety pin to prevent piece from unraveling while working the Trim and drop yarn to **wrong** side. Working in 🎥 Front Loops Only *(Fig. 3, page 30)*, join Contrasting Color with slip st in same st as joining; ch 1, (slip st in next dc, ch 1) around; join with slip st to first slip st, finish off. Place loop from safety pin onto crochet hook.

Rnd 2: Ch 3, working in 🎥 free loops of previous dc rnd *(Fig. 4a, page 30)*, dc in next dc and in each dc around; join with slip st to **both** loops of first dc.

Rnd 3: Ch 3, dc in both loops of next dc and each dc around; join with slip st to first dc.

SIZE SMALL ONLY
Rnds 4 and 5: Repeat Rnds 1 and 2; at end of Rnd 5, finish off.

SIZE MEDIUM ONLY
Rnds 4-6: Repeat Rnds 1-3; at end of Rnd 6, finish off.

SIZE LARGE ONLY
Rnds 4-8: Repeat Rnds 1-3 once, then repeat Rnds 1 and 2 once **more**; at end of Rnd 8, finish off.

SIZE EXTRA LARGE ONLY
Rnds 4-10: Repeat Rnds 1-3 twice, then repeat Rnd 3 once **more**; at end of Rnd 10, finish off.

HEEL
Row 1: Fold Toe in half with tip pointing up; with **right** side facing, join Main Color with slip st in dc at fold on last rnd of Foot; ch 3, dc in next dc and in each dc around; do **not** join: 21{23-25-27} dc.

Rows 2 thru 6{6-7-7}: Ch 3, turn; dc in next dc and in each dc across.

Joining: Fold last row in half with **right** side together. Working through **both** loops of both layers, slip st in each st across; finish off.

TOP TRIM
With **right** side facing, join Contrasting Color with slip st at seam; ch 1, (slip st, ch 1) evenly in end of rows around opening; join with slip st to first slip st, finish off.

POM-POM
Make a small 🎥 pom-pom *(Figs. A-C, page 8)* and sew to the tip of the Toe or at the top of the heel.

SOCK CUFF (Make 2)

The Sock Cuff is a separate piece that can be made for extra warmth.

With Color A, ch 20{24-28-32}; being careful **not** to twist ch, join with slip st to form a ring.

Rnd 1: Ch 3 (**counts as first dc, now and throughout**), dc in back ridge of next ch and each ch around (**Fig. 2, page 30**); join with slip st to first dc: 20{24-28-32} dc.

The mock ribbing is formed by alternating working in Back Loop Only (**abbreviated BLO**) and Front Loop Only (**abbreviated FLO**) (**Fig. 3, page 30**).

Rnd 2: Ch 3, dc in BLO of next dc, (dc in FLO of next dc, dc in BLO of next dc) around; drop Color A (do **not** cut yarn), changing to Color B, join with slip st to first dc (**Fig. 8, page 31**).

Rnd 3: Ch 1, sc in same st as joining, sc in BLO of next dc, (sc in FLO of next dc, sc in BLO of next dc) around; drop Color B, changing to Color A, join with slip st to first sc.

Rnd 4: Ch 3, dc in BLO of next sc, (dc in FLO of next sc, dc in BLO of next sc) around; join with slip st to first dc.

SIZE SMALL & SIZE MEDIUM

Rnds 5 and 6: Repeat Rnds 2 and 3; at end of Rnd 6 do **not** change colors, finish off.

SIZE LARGE & SIZE EXTRA LARGE

Rnds 5-9: Repeat Rnds 2-4 once, then repeat Rnds 2 and 3 once **more**; at end of Rnd 9, do **not** change colors, finish off.

Designs by Cathy Hardy.

POM-POMS

Cut a piece of cardboard 3" (7.5 cm) wide and as long as you want the diameter of your finished pom-pom to be.

Wind the yarn around the cardboard until it is approximately ½" (12 mm) thick in the middle (**Fig. A**).

Carefully slip the yarn off the cardboard and firmly tie an 18" (45.5 cm) length of yarn around the middle (**Fig. B**). Leave yarn ends long enough to attach the pom-pom.

Cut the loops on both ends and trim the pom-pom into a smooth ball (**Fig. C**).

Fig. A

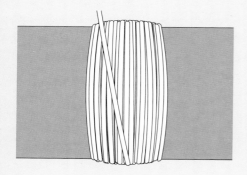

Fig. B

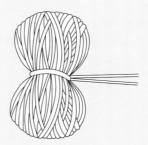

Fig. C

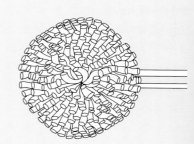

Striped Toe Slippers

■■□□ EASY +

SHOPPING LIST

Yarn (Medium Weight) 🧶**4**
- ☐ Black - 85{100-115-120} yards/77.5{91-105-110} meters
- ☐ Grey - 55{55-55-70} yards/ 50.5{50.5-50.5-64} meters

Crochet Hook
- ☐ Size G (4 mm) **or** size needed for gauge

Additional Supplies
- ☐ Yarn needle

SIZE INFORMATION

Adult Size	Finished Length	
Small	9"	(23 cm)
Medium	9¾"	(25 cm)
Large	10½"	(26.5 cm)
Extra Large	11"	(28 cm)

Size Note: We have printed the instructions for the sizes in different colors to make it easier for you to find:
- Size Small in Blue
- Size Medium in Pink
- Size Large in Green
- Size Extra Large in Purple

Instructions in Black apply to all sizes.

GAUGE INFORMATION

In Toe pattern, 11 sts = 3" (7.5 cm), 6 rows/rnds = 2" (5 cm)

Gauge Swatch: 3" wide x 2" high (7.5 cm x 5 cm)

With Grey, ch 12.

Row 1: Hdc in third ch from hook **(2 skipped chs count as first hdc)** and in each ch across: 11 hdc.

Row 2: Ch 1, turn; sc in each hdc across.

Row 3: Ch 2 **(counts as first hdc)**, turn; hdc in next sc and in each sc across.

Rows 4-6: Repeat Rows 2 and 3 once, then repeat Row 2 once **more**. Finish off.

SLIPPER (Make 2)
TOE

Rnd 1 (Right side)**:** With Grey, 🎥 make an adjustable loop to form a ring *(Figs. 1a-d, page 29)*; work 8{9-10-11} hdc in ring; drop Grey (do **not** cut yarn), 🎥 changing to Black, join with slip st to first hdc *(Fig. 8, page 31)*.

Note: Loop a short piece of yarn around any stitch to mark Rnd 1 as **right** side.

Rnd 2: Ch 1, 2 sc in each hdc around; drop Black, with Grey, join with slip st to first sc: 16{18-20-22} sc.

Rnd 3: Ch 2 **(counts as first hdc, now and throughout)**, hdc in next sc and in each sc around; drop Grey, with Black, join with slip st to first hdc.

Rnd 4: Ch 1, 2 sc in same st as joining, sc in next hdc, (2 sc in next hdc, sc in next hdc) around; drop Black, with Grey, join with slip st to first sc: 24{27-30-33} sc.

Rnd 5: Ch 2, hdc in next sc and in each sc around; drop Grey, with Black, join with slip st to first hdc.

Rnd 6: Ch 1, 2 sc in same st as joining, sc in next 2 hdc, (2 sc in next hdc, sc in next 2 hdc) around; drop Black, with Grey, join with slip st to first sc: 32{36-40-44} sc.

Rnd 7: Ch 2, hdc in next sc and in each sc around; drop Grey, with Black, join with slip st to first hdc.

Rnd 8: Ch 1, sc in each hdc around; drop Black, with Grey, join with slip st to first sc.

Rnds 9 thru 14{14-16-18}: Repeat Rnds 7 and 8, 3{3-4-5} times; at end of last rnd, cut Black.

Rnd 15{15-17-19}: Ch 2, hdc in next sc and in each sc around; join with slip st to first hdc, finish off.

HEEL

Row 1: With **right** side facing,  join Black with sc in ninth hdc **before** joining slip st *(see Joining With Sc, page 29)*; sc in next 23{25-27-29} hdc, leave remaining 8{10-12-14} hdc unworked: 24{26-28-30} sc.

Rows 2 thru 11{13-13-13}: Ch 1, turn; sc in Back Loop Only of each sc across *(Fig. 3, page 30)*.

Next 4 Rows: Ch 1, turn; working in Back Loops Only, sc in each sc across to last sc, 2 sc in last sc: 28{30-32-34} sc.

Finish off leaving a long end for sewing.

Fold last row in half with **wrong** side together. Using long end and working through **both** loops of both layers, whipstitch back seam *(Fig. 9a, page 31)*.

EDGING

With **right** side facing, join Grey with slip st in back seam; ch 1, sc in end of each row across Heel; sc in next 1{1-2-3} hdc on Toe, hdc in next 1{2-2-2} hdc, dc in next 4 hdc, hdc in next 1{2-2-2} hdc, sc in next 1{1-2-3} hdc and in end of each row across remainder of Heel; join with slip st to first sc, finish off.

Design by Ruth Shepherd.

Baby Moccasins

■■□□ **EASY**

Finished Size: 3½" (9 cm) long; fits shoe size 0 to 1½

SHOPPING LIST

Yarn (Super Fine Weight) **1**
☐ Brown - 75 yards (68.5 meters)
☐ Cream - small amount

Crochet Hook
☐ Size C (2.75 mm)
or size needed for gauge

Additional Supplies
☐ Tapestry needle
☐ Sewing needle
☐ Matching thread

GAUGE INFORMATION

12 dc and 6 rnds = 2" (5 cm)

Gauge Swatch: 1¾" wide x 2¼" long (4.5 cm x 5.75 cm)

Work same as Instep: 36 sc.

STITCH GUIDE

SINGLE CROCHET 2 TOGETHER
(abbreviated sc2tog)
Pull up a loop in each of next 2 sts, YO and draw through all 3 loops on hook.

SINGLE CROCHET 3 TOGETHER
(abbreviated sc3tog)
Pull up a loop in each of next 3 sts, YO and draw through all 4 loops on hook.

DOUBLE CROCHET 2 TOGETHER
(abbreviated dc2tog) (uses 2 sts)
★ YO, insert hook in **next** st, YO and pull up a loop, YO and draw through 2 loops on hook; repeat from ★ once **more**, YO and draw through all 3 loops on hook.

DOUBLE CROCHET 3 TOGETHER
(abbreviated dc3tog) (uses 3 sts)
★ YO, insert hook in **next** st, YO and pull up a loop, YO and draw through 2 loops on hook; repeat from ★ 2 times **more**, YO and draw through all 4 loops on hook.

MOCCASIN (Make 2)
INSTEP

With Brown, ch 9.

Rnd 1 (Right side)**:** 4 Dc in fourth ch from hook, dc in next 4 chs, 5 dc in last ch; working in free loops of beginning ch *(Fig. 4b, page 30)*, dc in next 4 chs; join with slip st to top of beginning ch: 18 sts.

Note: Loop a short piece of yarn around any stitch to mark Rnd 1 as **right** side.

Rnd 2: Ch 3 (**counts as first dc, now and throughout**), dc in same st as joining, 2 dc in each of next 4 dc, dc in next 4 dc, 2 dc in each of next 5 dc, dc in last 4 dc; join with slip st to first dc: 28 dc.

Rnd 3: Ch 1, 2 sc in same st as joining, (sc in next 2 dc, 2 sc in next dc) 3 times, sc in next 4 dc, 2 sc in next dc, (sc in next 2 dc, 2 sc in next dc) 3 times, sc in last 4 dc; join with slip st to first sc, do **not** finish off: 36 sc.

SIDES

Rnd 1: Ch 1, sc in Back Loop Only of first 2 sc *(Fig. 3, page 30)*, ch 24 **loosely**, skip next 10 sc, sc in Back Loop Only of each remaining sc; join with slip st to **both** loops of first sc: 26 sc.

Rnd 2: Ch 3, working in both loops of sc, dc in next sc and in next 10 chs, 2 dc in each of next 4 chs, dc in next 10 chs and in each sc around; join with slip st to first dc: 54 dc.

Rnds 3 and 4: Ch 3, dc in next dc and in each dc around; join with slip st to first dc, do **not** finish off.

SOLE

Rnd 1: Ch 3, working in Back Loops Only, dc in next 14 dc, dc2tog twice, dc in next 22 dc, dc3tog twice, dc in last 7 dc; join with slip st to **both** loops of first dc: 48 sts.

Rnd 2: Ch 1, working in both loops, sc in first 14 sts, sc2tog twice, sc in next 20 sts, sc2tog twice, sc in last 6 sts; join with slip st to first sc: 44 sts.

Rnd 3: Ch 1, sc in first 12 sts, sc2tog, sc3tog, sc in next 17 sts, sc2tog, sc3tog, sc in last 5 sts; join with slip st to first sc, finish off: 38 sts.

Fold Sole in half with **wrong** side together; using Brown, matching sts, and working through **both** loops of both layers, whipstitch bottom seam *(Fig. 9a, page 31)*.

TRIM

Using photo as a guide and Cream, add trim by working in same manner as whipstitch, working in free loops of each ch across ch-24 on Rnd 1 of Sides, then in each st around Instep working in free loops *(Fig. 4a, page 30)* and in unworked sts.

Work in same manner around bottom edge of Sides.

Design by Terry Kimbrough.

Globetrotters

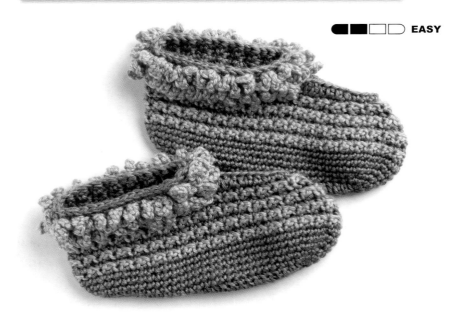

■■□□ **EASY**

SHOPPING LIST

Yarn (Medium Weight) 4
[5 ounces, 251 yards
(142 grams, 230 meters) per skein]:
☐ Main Color - 1 skein
☐ Contrasting Color - 1 skein

Crochet Hook
☐ Size Small - size G (4 mm)
☐ Size Medium - size H (5 mm)
☐ Size Large - size I (5.5 mm)
  or size needed for gauge

Additional Supplies
☐ Safety pin
☐ Yarn needle

SIZE INFORMATION

Adult Size	Finished Length	
Small	9"	(23 cm)
Medium	9½"	(24 cm)
Large	10"	(25.5 cm)

Size Note: We have printed the gauges for the sizes in different colors to make it easier for you:
• Size Small in Blue
• Size Medium in Pink
• Size Large in Green
Instructions in Black apply to all sizes.

GAUGE INFORMATION

In pattern,
  15{14-13} sts and 16{15-14} rnds/
  rows = 4" (10 cm)
Gauge Swatch: 4" (10 cm) square
With Main Color, ch 16{15-14}.
Row 1: Sc in second ch from hook
and in each ch across: 15{14-13} sc.
Rows 2 thru 16{15-14}: Ch 1, turn; sc
in each sc across.
Finish off.

STITCH GUIDE

🎥 **RIGHT DECREASE** (uses 2 sts)
Pull up a loop in next sc, YO, working **behind** next ch, insert hook in skipped st one rnd **below**, YO and pull up a loop, YO and draw through 2 loops on hook, YO and draw through all 3 loops on hook.

🎥 **LEFT DECREASE** (uses 2 sts)
YO, working **behind** next ch, insert hook in skipped st one rnd **below**, YO and pull up a loop, YO and draw through 2 loops on hook, pull up a loop in next sc, YO and draw through all 3 loops on hook.

SLIPPER (Make 2)
SOLE
With Main Color, ch 24.

Rnd 1 (Right side)**:** 2 Sc in second ch from hook, sc in next 9 chs, hdc in next 3 chs, dc in next 7 chs, 2 dc in next ch, hdc in next ch, 5 sc in last ch (toe); working in 🎥 free loops of beginning ch (*Fig. 4b, page 30*), hdc in next ch, 2 dc in next ch, dc in next 7 chs, hdc in next 3 chs, sc in next 9 chs, 2 sc in same ch as first sc; do **not** join, 🎥 place marker to indicate beginning of rnd (*see Markers, page 29*): 53 sts.

Note: Loop a short piece of yarn around any stitch to mark Rnd 1 as **right** side.

Rnd 2: 2 Sc in each of next 2 sc, sc in next 22 sts, 2 sc in next sc, (sc in next sc, 2 sc in next sc) twice, sc in next 22 sts, 2 sc in each of next 2 sc: 60 sc.

Rnd 3: Sc in next sc, 2 sc in next sc, sc in next 23 sc, 2 sc in next sc, (sc in next 2 sc, 2 sc in next sc) 3 times, sc in next 23 sc, 2 sc in next sc, sc in next sc: 66 sc.

Rnd 4: Sc in next sc, 2 sc in next sc, sc in next 26 sc, 2 sc in next sc, (sc in next 2 sc, 2 sc in next sc) 3 times, sc in next 26 sc, 2 sc in next sc, sc in next sc: 72 sc.

Rnd 5: Sc in next 33 sc, 2 sc in next sc, sc in next 4 sc, 2 sc in next sc, sc in next 33 sc; do **not** finish off: 74 sc.

SIDES

Rnd 1: Sc in each sc around; slip st in next sc to join, remove marker and 📹 place loop from hook onto safety pin to prevent piece from unraveling while working the next rnd.

Always drop yarn to **wrong** side.

Rnd 2: With **wrong** side facing, 📹 join Contrasting Color with sc in sc **before** joining *(see Joining With Sc, page 29)*; ch 1, skip next st, ★ sc in next sc, ch 1, skip next sc; repeat from ★ around; join with slip st to first sc, finish off: 37 sc and 37 chs.

Rnd 3: With **right** side facing, place loop from safety pin onto crochet hook; ch 3 **(counts as first dc, now and throughout)**, sc in next sc, ★ 📹 working behind next ch *(Fig. 7, page 31)*, dc in skipped sc one rnd **below**, sc in next sc; repeat from ★ around; join with slip st to first dc, place loop from hook onto safety pin: 74 sts.

Rnd 4: With **wrong** side facing, join Contrasting Color with sc in sc **before** joining; ch 1, skip next dc, ★ sc in next st, ch 1, skip next st; repeat from ★ around; join with slip st to first sc, finish off: 37 sc and 37 chs.

Rnd 5: With **right** side facing, place loop from safety pin onto crochet hook; ch 3, (sc in next sc, working **behind** next ch, dc in skipped dc one rnd **below**) 13 times, (sc in next sc, work Left Decrease, working **behind** next ch, dc in skipped dc one rnd **below**) 3 times, (work Right Decrease, sc in next sc, working **behind** next ch, dc in skipped dc one rnd **below**) 3 times, sc in next sc, (working **behind** next ch, dc in skipped dc one rnd **below**, sc in next sc) 11 times; join with slip st to first dc, place loop from hook onto safety pin: 68 sts.

Rnd 6: Repeat Rnd 4: 34 sc and 34 chs.

Rnd 7: With **right** side facing, place loop from safety pin onto crochet hook; ch 3, sc in next sc, (working **behind** next ch, dc in skipped dc one rnd **below**, sc in next sc) 11 times, (working **behind** next ch, dc in skipped dc one rnd **below**, work Right Decrease, sc in next sc) 3 times, (work Left Decrease, working **behind** next ch, dc in skipped st one rnd **below**, sc in next sc) 3 times, (working **behind** next ch, dc in skipped dc one rnd **below**, sc in next sc) 10 times; join with slip st to first dc, place loop from hook onto safety pin: 62 sts.

Rnd 8: Repeat Rnd 4: 31 sc and 31 chs.

Rnd 9: With **right** side facing, place loop from safety pin onto crochet hook; ch 3, (sc in next sc, working **behind** next ch, dc in skipped dc one rnd **below**) 9 times, place marker in last dc made for st placement, sc in next sc, (working **behind** next ch, dc in skipped st one rnd **below**, sc in next sc) twice, (working **behind** next ch, dc in skipped st one rnd **below**, sc in next sc, work Left Decrease) twice, (working **behind** next ch, dc in skipped st one rnd **below**, work Right Decrease, sc in next sc) twice, (working **behind** next ch, dc in skipped dc one rnd **below**, sc in next sc) 11 times; join with slip st to first dc, finish off: 58 sts.

INSTEP

With **right** side facing,  join Main Color with dc in marked dc *(see Joining With Dc, page 29)*; remove marker, dc in next 3 sts, hdc in next 4 sts, sc in next 3 sts, slip st in next 3 sts, sc in next 3 sts, hdc in next 4 sts, dc in next 4 sts, leave remaining 33 sts unworked; finish off leaving a long end for sewing: 25 sts.

Fold Instep in half with **wrong** side together. Using long end and working through **inside** loops only, whipstitch sts together *(Fig. 9b, page 31)*, beginning in first dc and last dc and ending in center slip st.

PLAIN CUFF

Rnd 1: With **right** side facing, join Main Color with sc in same st as joining on Rnd 9 of Sides; sc in next 17 sts, dc in same dc as first dc of Instep; working in end of rows on Instep, sc around post of first dc, sc in next joining and around post of next dc, dc in same dc as last dc of Instep; sc in last 15 sts; join with slip st to first sc: 38 sts.

Rnd 2: Slip st loosely in each st around; join with slip st to joining slip st, finish off.

RUFFLED CUFF

Rnd 1: With **wrong** side facing, join Contrasting Color with sc in sc **before** joining on Rnd 9 of Sides; ch 1, (skip next dc, sc in next sc, ch 1) 8 times, (sc around post of next dc of Instep, ch 1) twice, (sc in next sc, ch 1, skip next dc) 8 times; join with slip st to first sc, finish off: 19 sc and 19 chs.

Rnd 2: With **right** side facing and working **behind** Rnd 1, join Main Color with dc in same st as joining on Rnd 9 of Sides; sc in next sc, (working **behind** next ch, dc in skipped st one rnd **below**, sc in next sc) 8 times, working **behind** next ch, dc in same dc as first dc of Instep (on Rnd 9 of Sides), sc in next sc, working **behind** next ch, dc in joining one rnd **below**, sc in next sc, working **behind** next ch, dc in same dc as last dc of Instep (on Rnd 9 of Sides), sc in next sc, (working **behind** next ch, dc in skipped st one rnd **below**, sc in next sc) 7 times; join with slip st to first dc, place loop from hook onto safety pin: 38 sts.

Rnd 3: With **wrong** side facing, join Contrasting Color with sc in sc **before** joining; ch 1, skip next dc, ★ sc in next sc, ch 1, skip next dc; repeat from ★ around; join with slip st to first sc, finish off: 19 sc and 19 chs.

Rnd 4: With **right** side facing, place loop from safety pin onto crochet hook; ch 3, sc in next sc, (working **behind** next ch, dc in skipped dc one rnd **below**, sc in next sc) around; join with slip st to first dc: 38 sts.

Rnd 5: Slip st loosely in each st around; join with slip st to joining slip st, finish off.

RUFFLES

With **right** side facing, Sole toward you, and starting on Rnd 1 of Cuff, join Contrasting Color with slip st in Back Loop Only of ch at center of heel *(Fig. 3, page 30)*; † ch 7, slip st in Front Loop Only of same ch, ch 7, ★ slip st in Back Loop Only of next ch, ch 7, slip st in Front Loop Only of same ch, ch 7; repeat from ★ around †; working on Rnd 3 of Cuff, slip st in Back Loop Only of ch above joining slip st, repeat from † to † once; join with slip st to **both** loops of first slip st on Rnd 3, finish off.

Design by Anne Halliday.

Lace Toe Cross-overs

Optional Sock Cuffs shown on page 17.

■■□□ **EASY**

SIZE INFORMATION

Adult Size	Finished Length	
Small	9"	(23 cm)
Medium	10"	(25.5 cm)
Large	11"	(28 cm)

Size Note: We have printed the instructions for the sizes in different colors to make it easier for you to find:
- Size Small in Blue
- Size Medium in Pink
- Size Large in Green

Instructions in Black apply to all sizes.

GAUGE INFORMATION

LACE TOE

With smaller size hook,
   18 dc and 9 rows = 4" (10 cm)
Gauge Swatch: 5½" wide x 5¼" high
   (14 cm x 13.25 cm)
Work same as Lace Toe: 25 dc.

SOLE

With larger size hook and holding
2 strands of Main Color together,
   14 hdc and 10 rows = 4" (10 cm)
Gauge Swatch: 4" (10 cm) square
With larger size hook and holding
2 strands of Main Color together,
ch 15.
Row 1: Hdc in second ch from hook
and in each ch across: 14 hdc.
Rows 2-10: Ch 1 (does **not** count as a
st), turn; hdc in each hdc across.
Finish off.

SLIPPER (Make 2)
LACE TOE

With smaller size hook and
Contrasting Color, ch 14.

Row 1 (Right side): 2 Sc in second ch
from hook, sc in next 11 chs, 2 sc in
last ch: 15 sc.

Note: Loop a short piece of yarn
around any stitch to mark Row 1 as
right side.

Row 2: Ch 3 **(counts as first dc, now
and throughout)**, turn; dc in first sc
(increase made), dc in next sc and in
each sc across to last sc, 2 dc in last sc:
17 dc.

Row 3: Ch 3, turn; dc in first 6 dc, ch 1, skip next dc, dc in next 3 dc, ch 1, skip next dc, dc in next 5 dc, 2 dc in last dc: 17 dc and 2 ch-1 sps.

Row 4: Ch 3, turn; dc in first 5 dc, ch 1, skip next dc, dc in next dc, dc in next ch-1 sp and in next dc, ch 5, skip next dc, dc in next dc, dc in next ch-1 sp and in next dc, ch 1, skip next dc, dc in next 4 dc, 2 dc in last dc: 18 dc and 3 sps.

Row 5: Ch 3, turn; dc in first 4 dc, ch 1, skip next dc, dc in next dc, dc in next ch-1 sp and in next dc, ch 4, skip next 2 dc, sc in next ch-5 sp, ch 4, skip next 2 dc, dc in next dc, dc in next ch-1 sp and in next dc, ch 1, skip next dc, dc in next 3 dc, 2 dc in last dc: 16 dc, 1 sc, and 4 sps.

Row 6: Ch 3, turn; dc in first 3 dc, ch 1, skip next dc, dc in next dc, dc in next ch-1 sp and in next dc, ch 4, skip next 2 dc and next 3 chs, sc in next ch, sc in next sc and in next ch, ch 4, skip next 3 chs and next 2 dc, dc in next dc, dc in next ch-1 sp and in next dc, ch 1, skip next dc, dc in next 2 dc, 2 dc in last dc: 14 dc, 3 sc, and 4 sps.

Row 7: Ch 3, turn; dc in next dc, ch 1, skip next dc, dc in next dc, dc in next ch-1 sp and in next dc, ch 4, skip next 2 dc and next 3 chs, sc in next ch, sc in next 3 sc and in next ch, ch 4, skip next 3 chs and next 2 dc, dc in next dc, dc in next ch-1 sp and in next dc, ch 1, skip next dc, dc in last 2 dc: 10 dc, 5 sc, and 4 sps.

Row 8: Ch 3, turn; dc in next dc, dc in next ch-1 sp and in next dc, ch 1, skip next dc, dc in next dc and in next 2 chs, ch 4, skip next 2 chs and next sc, sc in next 3 sc, ch 4, skip next sc and next 2 chs, dc in next 2 chs and in next dc, ch 1, skip next dc, dc in next dc, dc in next ch-1 sp and in last 2 dc: 14 dc, 3 sc, and 4 sps.

Row 9: Ch 3, turn; dc in next 3 dc, dc in next ch-1 sp and in next dc, ch 1, skip next dc, dc in next dc and in next 2 chs, ch 4, skip next 2 chs and next sc, sc in next sc, ch 4, skip next sc and next 2 chs, dc in next 2 chs and in next dc, ch 1, skip next dc, dc in next dc, dc in next ch-1 sp and in last 4 dc: 18 dc, 1 sc, and 4 sps.

Row 10: Ch 3, turn; dc in next 5 dc, dc in next ch-1 sp and in next dc, ch 1, skip next dc, dc in next dc and in next 2 chs, ch 1, skip next sc and next 2 chs, dc in next 2 chs and in next dc, ch 1, skip next dc, dc in next dc, dc in next ch-1 sp and in last 6 dc: 22 dc and 3 ch-1 sps.

Row 11: Ch 3, turn; dc in next 7 dc and in next ch-1 sp, ★ dc in next dc, ch 1, skip next dc, dc in next dc and in next ch-1 sp; repeat from ★ once **more**, dc in last 8 dc: 23 dc and 2 ch-1 sps.

Row 12: Ch 3, turn; dc in next dc and in each dc and each ch-1 sp across; finish off: 25 dc.

BODY

Row 1: With **right** side facing, join Main Color with slip st in first dc; ch 1, sc in same st, (dc in next dc, sc in next dc) across.

Row 2: Ch 3, turn; (sc in next dc, dc in next sc) across.

Row 3: Ch 1, turn; sc in first dc, (dc in next sc, sc in next dc) across.

Repeat Rows 2 and 3 until piece measures approximately 18½{21-23½}"/47{53.5-59.5} cm from beginning ch.

TOE SHAPING

Rows 1-6: Ch 2 (does **not** count as a st), turn; skip first st, dc in next st and in each st across to last 2 sts, skip next st, dc in last st: 13 dc.

Finish off.

SOLE

Place a marker on one long edge of piece, 9{10-11}"/23{25.5-28} cm from beginning ch and also same distance from last row.

Note: When making the second slipper, work the Sole on the opposite long edge so you´ll have a right and left Slipper.

Row 1: With **right** side of piece facing, using larger size hook, and holding 2 strands of Main Color together, leave one of the ends long for sewing and join yarn with slip st at first marker; ch 1, work 10{12-14} hdc evenly spaced across end of rows to next marker, remove markers.

Row 2: Ch 1, turn; hdc in each hdc across.

Repeat Row 2 until Sole measures approximately 9{9½-10¼}"/ 23{24-26} cm.

SIZE SMALL ONLY
Finish off.

SIZE MEDIUM ONLY
Last Row: Ch 1, turn; skip first hdc, hdc in next 9 hdc, skip next hdc, hdc in last hdc; finish off: 10 hdc.

SIZE LARGE ONLY
Next Row: Ch 1, turn; skip first hdc, hdc in next 11 hdc, skip next hdc, hdc in last hdc: 12 hdc.

Next Row: Ch 1, turn; hdc in each hdc across.

Last Row: Ch 1, turn; skip first hdc, hdc in next 9 hdc, skip next hdc, hdc in last hdc; finish off: 10 hdc.

ASSEMBLY

To form each slipper, the Lace Toe and Body are joined together across the width, then placed on top of the Sole and sewn together as follows:

Place a marker on long edge of Body opposite center of Sole to indicate back top edge of opening.

With the **wrong** side of the slipper facing up, place the end of the Body on top of the Sole with **right** side up, then place Lace Toe on top, also with **right** side up *(Fig. A)*.

Fig. A

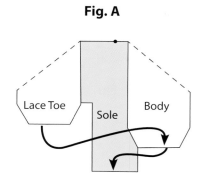

To create a double thickness for the toe, hold the top 2 layers together with edges even. Using Contrasting Color and working across the top of the Lace Toe and the corresponding row below, weave yarn through both layers to join the Lace Toe and the Body together.

Matching the end of all 3 layers, bring the marked edge of the Sole to the center of the slipper to form the opening.

Using one long end left at beginning of Sole and working through two layers, whipstitch across side of slipper to beginning of Lace Toe *(Figs. 9a & c, page 31)*; working through all 3 layers, whipstitch around toe to opposite side of Lace Toe; working through two layers, whipstitch across.

Fold down edge to form a cuff.

SOCK CUFF (Make 2)
The Sock Cuff is a separate piece that can be made for extra warmth.

Using smaller size hook and Contrasting Color, ch 40{46-48}; being careful **not** to twist ch, join with slip st to form a ring.

Rnd 1: Ch 3 (**counts as first dc, now and throughout**), dc in back ridge of next ch and each ch around *(Fig. 2, page 30)*; join with slip st to first dc: 40{46-48} dc.

The mock ribbing is formed by alternating working in Back Loop Only *(abbreviated BLO)* and Front Loop Only *(abbreviated FLO) (Fig. 3, page 30)*.

Rnd 2: Ch 3, dc in BLO of next dc, (dc in FLO of next dc, dc in BLO of next dc) around; join with slip st to first dc.

Repeat Rnd 2 for pattern 8{8-9} times **or** until Sock Cuff measures desired length.

Finish off.

Designs by Cathy Hardy.

2-Color Shells

Optional Sock Cuffs shown on page 19.

⬤⬤◻◻ **EASY**

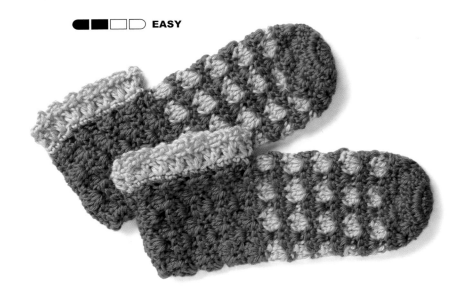

SHOPPING LIST

Yarn (Medium Weight) **4 MEDIUM**
[6 ounces, 315 yards
(170 grams, 288 meters) per skein]:
☐ Main Color - 1 skein
☐ Contrasting Color - 1 skein

Crochet Hook
☐ Size H (5 mm)
or size needed for gauge

SIZE INFORMATION

Size	Finished Length	
Child Small	6"	(15 cm)
Child Medium	7½"	(19 cm)
Child Large	8¼"	(21 cm)
Adult Small	9"	(23 cm)
Adult Medium	10"	(25.5 cm)
Adult Large	11"	(28 cm)

Size Note: We have printed the instructions for the sizes in different colors to make it easier for you to find:
• Child Size Small in Brown
• Child Size Medium in Purple
• Child Size Large in Red
• Adult Size Small in Blue
• Adult Size Medium in Pink
• Adult Size Large in Green
Instructions in Black apply to all sizes.

GAUGE INFORMATION

In pattern,
   8 sts = 2¼" (5.75 cm),
   6 rows/rnds = 2½" (6.25 cm)
Sock Cuff, 7 dc = 2" (5 cm)
Gauge Swatch: 3" wide x 2½" high
   (7.5 cm x 6.25 cm)
With Main Color, ch 12.
Row 1: Sc in second ch from hook, ★ skip next ch, 3 dc in next ch, skip next ch, sc in next ch; repeat from ★ once **more**, skip next ch, 2 dc in last ch: 11 sts.

Row 2: Ch 1, turn; working in 🎥 Back Loops Only (*Fig. 3, page 30*), sc in first dc, ★ skip next dc, 3 dc in next sc, skip next dc, sc in next dc; repeat from ★ once **more**, skip next dc, 2 dc in last sc.
Row 3: Ch 1, turn; working in both loops, sc in first dc, ★ skip next dc, 3 dc in next sc, skip next dc, sc in next dc; repeat from ★ once **more**, skip next dc, 2 dc in last sc.
Rows 4-6: Repeat Rows 2 and 3 once, then repeat Row 2 once **more**. Finish off.

SLIPPER (Make 2)
FOOT

Rnd 1 (Right side)**:** With Main Color, 🎥 make an adjustable loop to form a ring (*Figs. 1a-d, page 29*); ch 2 (**counts as first dc**), work {9-11-11} {13-13-15} dc in ring; join with slip st to first dc: {10-12-12}{14-14-16} dc.

Note: Loop a short piece of yarn around any stitch to mark Rnd 1 as **right** side.

Rnd 2: Ch 3 (**counts as first dc, now and throughout**), turn; dc in same st as joining, 2 dc in next dc and in each dc around; join with slip st to first dc: {20-24-24}{28-28-32} dc.

Rnd 3: Ch 1, turn; sc in same st as joining, skip next dc, 3 dc in next dc, skip next dc, ★ sc in next dc, skip next dc, 3 dc in next dc, skip next dc; repeat from ★ around; join with slip st to first sc: {5-6-6}{7-7-8} sc and {15-18-18}{21-21-24} dc.

Rnd 4: Ch 3, turn; dc in same st as joining, skip next dc, sc in next dc, skip next dc, ★ 3 dc in next sc, skip next dc, sc in next dc, skip next dc; repeat from ★ around, dc in same st as first dc; drop Main Color (do **not** cut yarn),  changing to Contrasting Color, join with slip st to first dc *(Fig. 8, page 31)*.

Rnd 5: Ch 1, turn; sc in same st as joining, skip next dc, working in Back Loops Only *(Fig. 3, page 30)*, 3 dc in next sc, skip next dc, ★ sc in next dc, skip next dc, 3 dc in next sc, skip next dc; repeat from ★ around; drop Contrasting Color, with Main Color, join with slip st to **both** loops of first sc.

Repeat Rnd 4 (working in both loops) and Rnd 5 (working in Back Loops Only), {1-3-4}{4-5-5} time(s).

Cut Contrasting Color.

Repeat Rnd 4, joining without changing colors; finish off.

HEEL

Row 1: With **right** side facing and working in Back Loops Only, skip first {10-10-10}{14-14-18} sts and join Main Color with slip st in next sc (center front); ch 3, skip next dc, sc in next dc, skip next dc, ★ 3 dc in next sc, skip next dc, sc in next dc, skip next dc; repeat from ★ around, dc in same st as joining; do **not** join: {19-23-23} {27-27-31} sts.

Row 2: Ch 1, turn; working in both loops, sc in first dc, 2 dc in next sc, skip next dc, sc in next dc, ★ skip next dc, 3 dc in next sc, skip next dc, sc in next dc; repeat from ★ across to last 3 sts, skip next dc, 2 dc in next sc, sc in last dc.

Row 3: Ch 3, turn; working in Back Loops Only, sc in next dc, ★ skip next dc, 3 dc in next sc, skip next dc, sc in next dc; repeat from ★ across to last sc, dc in last sc.

Repeat Rows 2 and 3, {1-1-1} {2-2-3} time(s); then repeat Row 2 once **more**.

Joining: Fold last row in half with **right** side together. Working through both loops of both layers, slip st in each st across; finish off.

EDGING

Rnd 1: With **right** side facing, join Contrasting Color with slip st in seam; ch 1, work {22-22-22}{30-30-38} sc evenly spaced across end of rows; join with slip st to first sc.

Rnd 2: Ch 4 (**counts as first dc plus ch 1**), dc in same st as joining, skip next sc, ★ (dc, ch 1, dc) in next sc, skip next sc; repeat from ★ around; join with slip st to first dc: {11-11-11} {15-15-19} ch-1 sps.

Rnd 3: (Slip st in next ch-1 sp, ch 4) around; join with slip st to first slip st, finish off.

SOCK CUFF (Make 2)

The Sock Cuff is a separate piece that can be made for extra warmth.

Using Contrasting Color, ch {20-24-28} {32-36-38}; being careful **not** to twist ch, join with slip st to form a ring.

Rnd 1: Ch 3 (**counts as first dc, now and throughout**), dc in back ridge of next ch and each ch around *(Fig. 2, page 30)*; join with slip st to first dc: {20-24-28}{32-36-38} dc.

The mock ribbing is formed by alternating working in Back Loop Only *(abbreviated BLO)* and Front Loop Only *(abbreviated FLO)* *(Fig. 3, page 30)*.

Rnd 2: Ch 3, dc in BLO of next dc, (dc in FLO of next dc, dc in BLO of next dc) around; join with slip st to first dc.

Repeat Rnd 2 for pattern {2-3-4} {5-5-6} times **or** until Sock Cuff measures desired length.

Finish off.

Designs by Cathy Hardy.

19

Toddler Slippers

▰▰▱▱ **EASY**

SIZE INFORMATION

Size	Finished Length	
Small	4"	(10 cm)
Medium	4½"	(11.5 cm)
Large	5"	(12.5 cm)

Size Note: We have printed the gauges for the sizes in different colors to make it easier for you:
• Size Small in Brown
• Size Medium in Purple
• Size Large in Red
Instructions in Black apply to all sizes.

GAUGE INFORMATION

Gauge Swatch: 2{2¼-2½}"/
  5{5.75-6.25} cm
Work same as Square.

SLIPPER (Make 2)
SQUARE (Make 3)
Ch 4; join with slip st to form a ring.

Rnd 1 (Right side)**:** Ch 2 (**counts as first hdc, now and throughout**), 2 hdc in ring, ch 2, (3 hdc in ring, ch 2) 3 times; join with slip st to first hdc: 12 hdc and 4 corner ch-2 sps.

Note: Loop a short piece of yarn around any stitch to mark Rnd 1 as **right** side.

Rnd 2: Ch 2, hdc in next 2 hdc, (2 hdc, ch 1, 2 hdc) in next ch-2 sp, ★ hdc in next 3 hdc, (2 hdc, ch 1, 2 hdc) in next ch-2 sp; repeat from ★ 2 times **more**; join with slip st to first hdc, finish off: 28 hdc and 4 corner ch-1 sps.

With **wrong** sides together and working through **inside** loops only, 🎥 whipstitch two Squares together along one edge for Sole (*Fig. 9b, page 31*).

SIDES

Rnd 1: Ch 12 **loosely**; with **right** side of remaining Square facing (Instep) and working in  Back Loops Only of each hdc and in each ch *(Fig. 3, page 30)*, sc in first hdc after any corner ch-1 sp; sc in next 24 sts, ch 11 **loosely**; being careful not to twist chs, join with slip st to first ch of beginning ch-12: 25 sc and 23 chs.

Rnd 2: Ch 1, sc in each ch and in both loops of each sc around, place marker in last ch worked into for Cuff placement; join with slip st to first sc: 48 sc.

Rnd 3: Ch 1, sc in each sc around; join with slip st to first sc, finish off leaving a long end for sewing.

Using long end, lining up Instep Square with one Square on Sole, and working through **both** loops of sts on **both** pieces, whipstitch Sides to Sole *(Fig. 9a, page 31)*.

CUFF

Rnd 1: With **right** side facing, working in free loops of chs on Rnd 1 of Sides *(Fig. 4b, page 30)* and in unworked sts on Instep, join yarn with slip st in marked ch; ch 3 (**counts as first hdc plus ch 1, now and throughout**), (skip next ch, hdc in next ch, ch 1) 5 times, (hdc in next hdc, ch 1, skip next hdc) 3 times, hdc in next ch, ch 1, (hdc in next ch, ch 1, skip next ch) 6 times; join with slip st to first hdc: 16 ch-1 sps.

Rnd 2: Ch 3, skip next ch, ★ hdc in next hdc, ch 1, skip next ch; repeat from ★ around; join with slip st to first hdc.

The Ruffle is formed by working around the post of each hdc *(Fig. A)* and in ch-1 sps on previous 2 rnds.

Fig. A

Ruffle: Slip st in first ch-1 sp, ch 2, hdc in same sp, 2 hdc around post of next hdc, 2 hdc in next sp on Rnd 1, 2 hdc around post of next hdc on Rnd 2, ★ 2 hdc in next ch-1 sp, 2 hdc around post of next hdc, 2 hdc in next sp on Rnd 1, 2 hdc around post of next hdc on Rnd 2; repeat from ★ around; join with slip st to first hdc, finish off.

TIE

Ch 4, slip st in fourth ch from hook, ch 65, slip st in fourth ch from hook; finish off.

Weave Tie through ch-1 sps on Rnd 1 of Cuff.

Design by Ruth Shepherd.

Pretty Roses

◼◼◻◻ **EASY**

SHOPPING LIST

Yarn (Medium Weight) **[4]**
[3.5 ounces, 170 yards
(100 grams, 156 meters) per skein]:
☐ 1 skein

Crochet Hook
☐ Size H (5 mm)
 or size needed for gauge

Additional Supplies
☐ Yarn needle

SIZE INFORMATION

Size	Finished Length	
Child Medium	7½"	(19 cm)
Child Large	8"	(20.5 cm)
Child X-Large	8½"	(21.5 cm)
Adult Small	9"	(23 cm)
Adult Medium	9½"	(24 cm)
Adult Large	10"	(25.5 cm)

Size Note: We have printed the instructions for the sizes in different colors to make it easier for you to find:
• Child Size Medium in Brown
• Child Size Large in Purple
• Child Size X-Large in Red
• Adult Size Small in Blue
• Adult Size Medium in Pink
• Adult Size Large in Green
Instructions in Black apply to all sizes.

GAUGE INFORMATION
In pattern,
 16 hdc and 8 rows = 4" (10 cm)
Gauge Swatch: 4" (10 cm) square
Ch 17.
Row 1: Hdc in third ch from hook
(2 skipped chs count as first hdc) and
in each ch across: 16 hdc.
Rows 2-8: Ch 2 **(counts as first hdc)**,
turn; working in 🎥 Back Loops Only
(Fig. 3, page 30), hdc in next hdc and
in each hdc across.
Finish off.

SLIPPER (Make 2)
BODY
Leaving a long end for sewing,
ch {31-33-35}{37-39-41}.

Row 1: Hdc in 🎥 back ridge **(Fig. 2,
page 30)** of third ch from hook
(2 skipped chs count as first hdc) and
each ch across: {30-32-34}
{36-38-40} hdc.

Row 2: Ch 2 **(counts as first hdc, now
and throughout)**, turn; working in
🎥 Back Loops Only **(Fig. 3, page 30)**,
hdc in next hdc and in each hdc
across.

Repeat Row 2 for pattern until Body
measures approximately 7" (18 cm)
for Child sizes **or** 9" (23 cm) for Adult
sizes from beginning ch, **or** to desired
measurement around foot.

Joining Row (Instep): Ch 1, turn;
fold Body in half lengthwise having
beginning ch behind last row,
working in Back Loops Only of last
row and in 🎥 free loops of beginning
ch **(Fig. 4b, page 30)**, sc in first
{11-13-15}{15-15-15} sts, leave
remaining sts unworked to form
opening; finish off.

Thread yarn needle with an 18" (45.5 cm) length and weave through end of rows at toe; gather tightly and secure ends.

Using long end, whipstitch heel seam, matching rows *(Fig. 9c, page 31)*.

FLOWER
Ch 24.

Row 1: Dc in fourth ch from hook, ★ ch 2, skip next ch, dc in next ch; repeat from ★ across: 11 dc and 10 ch-2 sps.

Row 2 (Right side)**:** Ch 1, turn; 5 dc in first ch-2 sp (**petal made**), sc in next dc, ★ 5 dc in next ch-2 sp, sc in next dc; repeat from ★ 8 times **more**, 5 dc around ch-3 on end of Row 1, sc in free loop of next ch (ch at base of first dc on Row 1); finish off leaving a long end for sewing: 11 petals.

Note: Loop a short piece of yarn around any stitch to mark Row 2 as **right** side.

With **right** side facing, loosely wrap petals around last petal made to form flower; tack bottom of petals in place. Sew Flower securely to Instep of Slipper.

Design by Mary A. Watkins.

Flower Grannies

◼◼◻◻ **EASY**

SHOPPING LIST
Yarn (Medium Weight) **4** MEDIUM
[3.5 ounces, 170 yards (100 grams, 156 meters) per skein]:
- ☐ Black - 1 skein
- ☐ Green - 55 yards (50.5 meters)
- ☐ Rose - 35 yards (32 meters)

Crochet Hook
- ☐ Size Small - size E (3.5 mm)
- ☐ Size Medium - size E (3.5 mm)
- ☐ Size Large - size F (3.75 mm)
  or size needed for gauge

Additional Supplies
- ☐ Yarn needle

SIZE INFORMATION

Adult Size	Length	
Small	9"	(23 cm)
Medium	9½"	(24 cm)
Large	10"	(25.5 cm)

Size Note: We have printed the instructions for the sizes in different colors to make it easier for you to find:
- Size Small in Blue
- Size Medium in Pink
- Size Large in Green

Instructions in Black apply to all sizes.

GAUGE INFORMATION

Gauge Swatch: 3½{3¾-4½}"/
9{9.5-11.5} cm
Work same as Square.

SLIPPER (Make 2)
SQUARE (Make 6)

Rnd 1 (Right side)**:** With Rose,
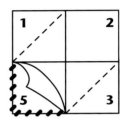 make an adjustable loop to form a
ring *(Figs. 1a-d, page 29)*; ch 3 **(counts
as first dc, now and throughout)**,
2 dc in ring, ch 1, (3 dc in ring, ch 1) 3
times; join with slip st to first dc,
finish off: 12 dc and 4 ch-1 sps.

Note: Loop a short piece of yarn
around any stitch to mark Rnd 1 as
right side.

Rnd 2: With **right** side facing, join
Green with dc in any ch-1 sp *(see
Joining With Dc, page 29)*; (2 dc, ch 1,
3 dc) in same sp, (3 dc, ch 1, 3 dc) in
next 3 ch-1 sps; join with slip st to first
dc, finish off: 24 dc and 4 ch-1 sps.

Rnd 3: With **right** side facing, join
Black with dc in any ch-1 sp; (2 dc,
ch 1, 3 dc) in same sp, skip next 3 dc,
3 dc in sp before next dc *(Fig. 6,
page 31)*, ★ (3 dc, ch 1, 3 dc) in next
ch-1 sp, skip next 3 dc, 3 dc in sp
before next dc; repeat from ★ 2 times
more; join with slip st to first dc,
do **not** finish off: 36 dc and 4 ch-1 sps.

SIZE SMALL ONLY

Rnd 4: Ch 1, sc in same st as joining
and in next 2 dc, 3 sc in next ch-1 sp,
(sc in next 9 dc, 3 sc in next ch-1 sp) 3
times, sc in last 6 dc; join with slip st
to first sc, finish off: 48 sc.

SIZE MEDIUM ONLY

Rnd 4: Ch 2 **(counts as first hdc)**, hdc
in next 2 dc, 3 hdc in next ch-1 sp,
(hdc in next 9 dc, 3 hdc in next
ch-1 sp) 3 times, hdc in last 6 dc; join
with slip st to first hdc, finish off:
48 hdc.

SIZE LARGE ONLY

Rnd 4: Slip st in next 2 dc and in next
ch-1 sp, ch 3, (2 dc, ch 1, 3 dc) in same
sp, (skip next 3 dc, 3 dc in sp **before**
next dc) twice, ★ (3 dc, ch 1, 3 dc) in
next ch-1 sp, (skip next 3 dc, 3 dc in sp
before next dc) twice; repeat from ★
2 times **more**; join with slip st to first
dc, finish off: 48 dc and 4 ch-1 sps.

ASSEMBLY

With Black, **wrong** sides together,
and working through **inside** loops
only, whipstitch Squares together
(Fig. 9b, page 31), forming 2 vertical
strips of 2 Squares each; then
whipstitch strips together.

Form heel by joining Square 5 to
corner *(Fig. A)*; then form toe by
joining Square 6 to opposite corner
and to Square 1 and Square 3 *(Fig. B)*.

Fig. A

Fig. B

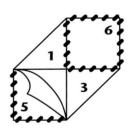

Design by Knit 'N' Purl Shop.

Baby Booties

Finished Size: 3½" (9 cm) long; fits shoe size 0 to 1½

SHOPPING LIST

Yarn (Super Fine Weight) 🧶**1**
☐ 115 yards (105 meters)
Crochet Hook
☐ Size C (2.75 mm)
or size needed for gauge
Additional Supplies
☐ Tapestry needle

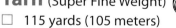

GAUGE INFORMATION

12 sts = 2" (5 cm)
Gauge Swatch: 2" (5 cm) diameter
Work same as Toe Motif: 29 tr.

STITCH GUIDE

📹 **TREBLE CROCHET**
(abbreviated tr)
YO twice, insert hook in sp indicated, YO and pull up a loop (4 loops on hook), (YO and draw through 2 loops on hook) 3 times.

📹 **BACK POST DOUBLE CROCHET**
(abbreviated BPdc)
YO, insert hook from **back** to **front** around post of dc indicated, YO and pull up a loop, (YO and draw through 2 loops on hook) twice **(Figs. 5a & b, page 30)**.

BOOTIE (Make 2)
SOLE
TOE MOTIF

Rnd 1 (Right side): 📹 Make an adjustable loop to form a ring **(Figs. 1a-d, page 29)**; ch 4 **(counts as first tr)**, work 28 tr in ring; join with slip st to first tr, finish off: 29 tr.

Note: Loop a short piece of yarn around any stitch to mark Rnd 1 as **right** side.

HEEL MOTIF

Rnd 1 (Right side): Make an adjustable loop to form a ring; ch 3 **(counts as first dc)**, work 11 dc in ring; hold Toe Motif behind Heel Motif with **wrong** sides together, slip st in any tr on **Toe Motif**, ★ dc in ring on **Heel Motif**, slip st in next tr on **Toe Motif**; repeat from ★ 2 times **more**, 9 dc in ring on **Heel Motif**; join with slip st to first dc, do **not** finish off: 24 dc.

SIDES

Rnd 1: Ch 1, sc in same st as joining and in next 11 dc, ch 1, sc in next 25 tr on Toe Motif, ch 1, sc in last 9 dc on Heel Motif; join with slip st to first sc: 46 sc and 2 chs.

Rnd 2: Ch 1, working in 📹 Back Loops Only **(Fig. 3, page 30)**, hdc in same st as joining and in next 11 sc, hdc in next ch and in next 25 sc, hdc in next ch and in last 9 sc; join with slip st to **both** loops of first hdc: 48 hdc.

Rnds 3-5: Ch 1, sc in both loops of each st around; join with slip st to first sc.

Rnd 6: Ch 2 (**counts as first hdc**), hdc in next 38 sc, place marker around last hdc made for Instep Motif placement, hdc in last 9 sc; join with slip st to first hdc, finish off.

INSTEP MOTIF

Rnd 1 (Right side)**:** Make an adjustable loop to form a ring; ch 2 (**counts as first dc**), work 2 dc in ring; hold Sides behind Instep Motif with **wrong** sides together, slip st in marked hdc, remove marker, dc in ring on **Instep Motif**, † skip next hdc on **Sides**, slip st in next hdc, dc in ring on **Instep Motif** †; repeat from † to † 4 times **more**, slip st in next hdc on **Sides**, dc in ring on **Instep Motif**,

repeat from † to † 7 times, leave remaining hdc on Sides unworked; join with slip st to first dc, finish off: 17 dc.

CUFF

Rnd 1 (Eyelet rnd)**:** With **right** side facing, join yarn with slip st in same st as joining on Rnd 6 of Sides; ch 3 (**counts as first dc**), dc in next 12 hdc, work BPdc around next 4 dc on Instep Motif, dc in next 9 hdc on Sides; join with slip st to first dc: 26 sts.

Rnds 2 and 3: Ch 2 (**counts as first hdc, now and throughout**), hdc in next st and in each st around; join with slip st to first hdc.

Rnds 4-6: Ch 1, sc in each st around; join with slip st to first sc.

Rnd 7: Ch 2, hdc in next sc and in each sc around; join with slip st to first hdc.

Rnd 8: Ch 1, sc in each hdc around; join with slip st to first sc, finish off.

TRIM

Holding Cuff toward you and working in  free loops of Rnd 1 on Sides (**Fig. 4a, page 30**), join yarn with slip st in any st; slip st in each st around; join with slip st to first slip st, finish off.

TIE

Holding 2 strands of yarn together, chain a 19" (48.5 cm) length; finish off. Weave Tie through Eyelet rnd of Cuff.

Design by Joye Steinle.

Sizing & Tips

CHOOSING YARN

Check the yarn label for washing instructions and purchase a yarn that will meet your needs. Some yarns are more durable and able to be laundered multiple times.

SLIPPER SIZING

When deciding which size slipper to make, consider the fit of the slipper. As long as the slippers are made from a yarn with elasticity, the fabric will have some give. You want the slippers to fit snug enough to stay on.

Measure the length of the foot (standing up). The slippers are based on this measurement.

Choose a finished slipper length the same length or slightly shorter than the length of the foot. Use the sizing charts, page 27, as a guide.

Also, it is very important to achieve the given gauge (*see Gauge, page 28*).

SIZING CHARTS

Size	Slipper Length	cm	Shoe Size
Baby	3½"	9	0 to 1½
Toddler			
Small	4"	10	2½ to 3½
Medium	4½"	11.5	4 to 5
Large	5"	12.5	5½ to 6½

Child Size	Slipper Length	cm	Shoe Size
Small	5¾" to 6"	14.5 to 15	8½ to 11
Medium	7" to 7½"	18 to 19	11½ to 13½
Large	8" to 8¼"	20.5 to 21	1 to 2½
Extra Large	8½" to 9"	21.5 to 23	3 to 5½

Adult Size	Slipper Length	cm	Shoe Size - Women	Shoe Size - Men
Small	9"	23	6½ to 7½	6
Medium	9½" to 10"	24 to 25.5	8 to 9½	6½ to 9½
Large	10" to 11"	25.5 to 28	9½ to 11½	9½ to 12
Extra Large	11"	28	12	12

NO SLIP FINISHING
PAINT
To provide traction on the bottom of each Slipper, rows of wavy lines or dots of dimensional fabric paint can be added to the bottom of your slippers as desired. Let the paint dry completely before wearing.

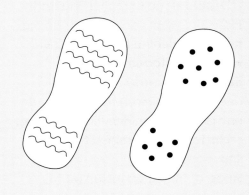

General Instructions

ABBREVIATIONS

BLO	Back Loop Only
BPdc	Back Post double crochet(s)
ch(s)	chain(s)
cm	centimeters
dc	double crochet(s)
dc2tog	double crochet 2 together
dc3tog	double crochet 3 together
FLO	Front Loop Only
hdc	half double crochet(s)
mm	millimeters
Rnd(s)	Round(s)
sc	single crochet(s)
sc2tog	single crochet 2 together
sc3tog	single crochet 3 together
sp(s)	space(s)
st(s)	stitch(es)
tr	treble crochet(s)
YO	yarn over

★ — work instructions following ★ as many **more** times as indicated in addition to the first time.

† to † — work all instructions from first † to second † **as many** times as specified.

( ) or [ ] — work enclosed instructions **as many** times as specified by the number immediately following **or** work all enclosed instructions in the stitch or space indicated **or** contains explanatory remarks.

colon (:) — the number(s) given after a colon at the end of a row or round denote(s) the number of stitches or spaces you should have on that row or round.

GAUGE

Exact gauge is **essential** for proper fit. Before beginning your project, make the sample swatch given in the individual instructions in the yarn and hook specified.

After completing the swatch, measure it, counting your stitches and rows or rounds carefully. If your swatch is larger or smaller than specified, **make another, changing hook size to get the correct gauge.** Keep trying until you find the size hook or needle that will give you the specified gauge.

CROCHET TERMINOLOGY

UNITED STATES	INTERNATIONAL
slip stitch (slip st) =	single crochet (sc)
single crochet (sc) =	double crochet (dc)
half double crochet (hdc) =	half treble crochet (htr)
double crochet (dc) =	treble crochet (tr)
treble crochet (tr) =	double treble crochet (dtr)
double treble crochet (dtr) =	triple treble crochet (ttr)
triple treble crochet (tr tr) =	quadruple treble crochet (qtr)
skip =	miss

Yarn Weight Symbol & Names	LACE 0	SUPER FINE 1	FINE 2	LIGHT 3	MEDIUM 4	BULKY 5	SUPER BULKY 6	JUMBO 7
Type of Yarns in Category	Fingering, size 10 crochet thread	Sock, Fingering, Baby	Sport, Baby	DK, Light Worsted	Worsted, Afghan, Aran	Chunky, Craft, Rug	Super Bulky, Roving	Jumbo, Roving
Crochet Gauge* Ranges in Single Crochet to 4" (10 cm)	32-42 sts**	21-32 sts	16-20 sts	12-17 sts	11-14 sts	8-11 sts	6-9 sts	5 sts and fewer
Advised Hook Size Range	Steel*** 6 to 8, Regular hook B-1	B-1 to E-4	E-4 to 7	7 to I-9	I-9 to K-10½	K-10½ to M/N-13	M/N-13 to Q	Q and larger

*GUIDELINES ONLY: The chart above reflects the most commonly used gauges and hook sizes for specific yarn categories.

** Lace weight yarns are usually crocheted with larger hooks to create lacy openwork patterns. Accordingly, a gauge range is difficult to determine. Always follow the gauge stated in your pattern.

*** Steel crochet hooks are sized differently from regular hooks–the higher the number, the smaller the hook, which is the reverse of regular hook sizing.

MARKERS

Markers are used to help distinguish the beginning of each round being worked. Place a 2" (5 cm) scrap piece of yarn before the first stitch of each round, moving the marker after each round is complete.

JOINING WITH SC

When instructed to join with sc, begin with a slip knot on hook. Insert hook in stitch or space indicated, YO and pull up a loop, YO and draw through both loops on hook.

JOINING WITH DC

When instructed to join with dc, begin with a slip knot on hook. YO, holding loop on hook, insert hook in stitch or space indicated, YO and pull up a loop (3 loops on hook), (YO and draw through 2 loops on hook) twice.

ADJUSTABLE LOOP

Wind the yarn around two fingers to form a ring *(Fig. 1a)*, slide the yarn off your fingers and grasp the strands at the top of the ring *(Fig. 1b)*. Insert the hook from **front** to **back** into the ring, pull up a loop, YO and draw through the loop on hook to lock the ring *(Fig. 1c)*.

Working around **both** strands, work stitches in the ring as specified, then pull the yarn end to close *(Fig. 1d)*.

Fig. 1a

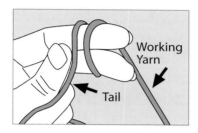

Fig. 1b

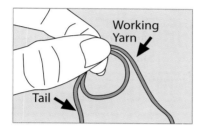

Fig. 1c

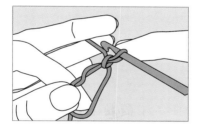

Fig. 1d

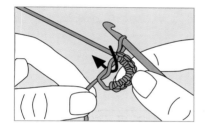

CROCHET HOOKS																
U.S.	B-1	C-2	D-3	E-4	F-5	G-6	7	H-8	I-9	J-10	K-10½	L-11	M/N-13	N/P-15	P/Q	Q	S
Metric - mm	2.25	2.75	3.25	3.5	3.75	4	4.5	5	5.5	6	6.5	8	9	10	15	16	19

◼◻◻◻ **BEGINNER**	Projects for first-time crocheters using basic stitches. Minimal shaping.
◼◼◻◻ **EASY**	Projects using yarn with basic stitches, repetitive stitch patterns, simple color changes, and simple shaping and finishing.
◼◼◼◻ **INTERMEDIATE**	Projects using a variety of techniques, such as basic lace patterns or color patterns, mid-level shaping and finishing.
◼◼◼◼ **EXPERIENCED**	Projects with intricate stitch patterns, techniques and dimension, such as non-repeating patterns, multi-color techniques, fine threads, small hooks, detailed shaping and refined finishing.

BACK RIDGE

Work only in loop(s) indicated by arrow *(Fig. 2)*.

Fig. 2

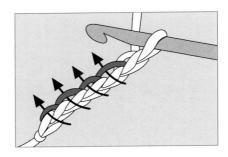

BACK OR FRONT LOOP ONLY

Work only in loop(s) indicated by arrow *(Fig. 3)*.

Fig. 3

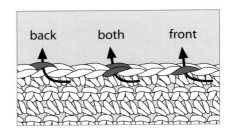

FREE LOOPS

After working in Back or Front Loops Only on a row or round, there will be a ridge of unused loops. These are called the free loops. Later, when instructed to work in the free loops of the same row or round, work in these loops *(Fig. 4a)*.

When instructed to work in free loops of a chain, work in loop indicated by arrow *(Fig. 4b)*.

Fig. 4a

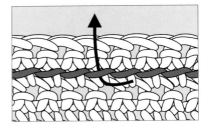

Fig. 4b

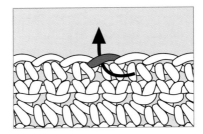

BACK POST DOUBLE CROCHET *(abbreviated BPdc)*

YO, insert hook from **back** to **front** around post of st indicated *(Fig. 5a)*, YO and pull up a loop (even with last st made) (3 loops on hook) *(Fig. 5b)*, (YO and draw through 2 loops on hook) twice. Skip st in front of BPdc.

Fig. 5a

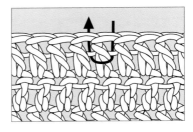

Fig. 5b

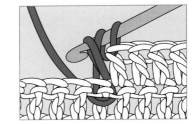

WORKING IN SPACE BEFORE A STITCH

When instructed to work in space **before** a stitch or in spaces **between** stitches, insert hook in space indicated by arrow *(Fig. 6)*.

Fig. 6

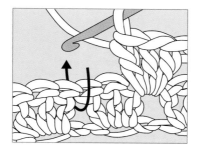

WORKING IN FRONT OF, AROUND, OR BEHIND A STITCH

Work in stitch or space indicated, inserting hook in direction of arrow *(Fig. 7)*.

Fig. 7

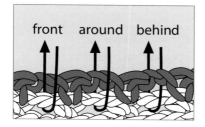

CHANGING COLORS

To change colors while joining with slip st, drop yarn to **wrong** side, insert hook in first st *(Fig. 8)*, hook new yarn and draw through st **and** loop on hook.

Fig. 8

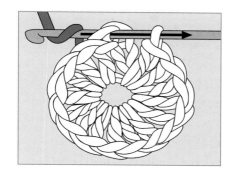

WHIPSTITCH

With **wrong** sides together, sew through both pieces once to secure the beginning of the seam, leaving an ample yarn end to weave in later. Insert the needle from **front** to **back** through **both** strands on each piece *(Fig. 9a)*, through **inside** loops only *(Fig. 9b)*, or through **2 strands** at end of rows *(Fig. 9c)*. Bring the needle around and insert it from **front** to **back** through the next strand(s) on both pieces. Repeat along the edge, being careful to match stitches and rows.

Fig. 9a

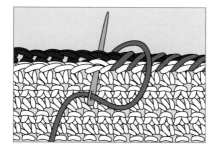

Fig. 9b

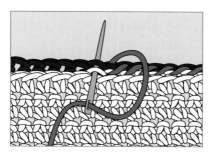

Fig. 9c

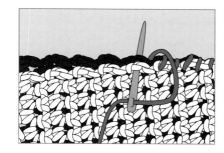

Yarn Information

The items in this book were made using a variety of yarn weights. Any brand of the specified weight yarn may be used. It is best to refer to the yardage/meters when determining how many skeins or balls to purchase. Remember, to arrive at the finished size, it is the GAUGE/TENSION that is important, not the brand of yarn.

For your convenience, listed below are the yarns used to create our photography models. Because yarn manufacturers make frequent changes in their product lines, you may sometimes find it necessary to use a substitute yarn or to search for the discontinued product at alternate suppliers (locally or online).

ELF SHOES
Caron® United™
Main Color - #6014 Navy
Contrasting Color - #6018 White &
  Navy Marl
Holiday option
Main Color - #6012 Fresh Green
Contrasting Color - #6008 Red
Sock Cuffs option
Color A - #6008 Red
Color B - #6011 Mustard

STRIPED TOE SLIPPERS
Red Heart® Super Saver®
Black - #312 Black
Grey - #341 Light Grey

BABY MOCCASINS
Patons® Kroy Socks FX
Brown - #57013 Cowboy Colors
Patons® Kroy Socks
Cream - #55008 Muslin

GLOBETROTTERS
Lion Brand® Heartland®
Plain Cuff
Main Color - #135 Yosemite
Contrasting Color - #109 Olympic
Ruffled Cuff
Main Color - #173 Everglades
Contrasting Color - #103 Denali

LACE TOE CROSS-OVERS
Red Heart® Cutie Pie™
Main Color - #0703 Tulip
Contrasting Color - #0010 Cotton

2-COLOR SHELLS
Caron® Simply Soft®
Main Color - #9770 Cool Green
Contrasting Color - #9780 Robin's Egg
Holiday option
Main Color - #9763 Harvest Red
Contrasting Color - #9701 White
Sock Cuff option
#9701 White

TODDLER SLIPPERS
Caron® Simply Soft® Paints™
#0016 Rainbow Bright

PRETTY ROSES
Lion Brand® Vanna's Choice® Baby
#139 Berrylicious

FLOWER GRANNIES
Lion Brand® Vanna's Choice®
Black - #153 Black
Green - #171 Fern
Rose - #112 Raspberry

BABY BOOTIES
Patons® Kroy Socks
#55705 Red

We have made every effort to ensure that these instructions are accurate and complete. We cannot, however, be responsible for human error, typographical mistakes, or variations in individual work.

Items made and instructions tested by Janet Akins.

Production Team: Instructional/Technical Writer - Cathy Hardy; Editorial Writer - Susan Frantz Wiles; Senior Graphic Artist - Lora Puls; Photo Stylist - Lori Wenger; and Photographer - Jason Masters.